WHAT ARE THE BOOKS OF SONG OF SONGS & LAMENTATIONS?

Kids' Guides to God's Word Series

What Are the Books of

SONG OF SONGS & LAMENTATIONS?

Michael Whitworth

ISBN 978-1-944704-79-7

Published by Start2Finish
Bend, Oregon 97702
start2finish.org

Printed in the United States of America
30 29 28 27 26   1 2 3 4 5

CONTENTS

A NOTE TO PARENTS

Song of Songs and Lamentations contain some of the Bible's most emotionally intense material. Song of Songs is love poetry that celebrates romantic desire and physical beauty, and Lamentations describes the devastating aftermath of war, including famine, violence, and profound grief. This book handles both with honesty and care, focusing on the theological themes and emotional truths without graphic detail, and always pointing young readers toward God's purposes. That said, every family is different, and you know your child best. I encourage you to read through this book before or alongside your young reader so you can address any questions that arise and have the kinds of conversations these remarkable biblical texts were meant to spark.

INTRODUCTION

What's the strongest emotion you've ever felt? Maybe it was the rush of being chosen first, of hearing someone say, "I want you on my team." Maybe it was the ache of losing someone: a grandparent who died, a friend who moved away, or a pet you'd had since you were little. Maybe it was the dizzy, terrifying, wonderful feeling of realizing that someone you cared about actually cared about you too. Or maybe it was the hollow emptiness of a day when everything went wrong and nobody seemed to notice.

Here's something most people don't expect about the Bible: it contains all of those feelings. Every single one. Not just in the stories, where characters experience them, but in two books that are made entirely of emotion, set to poetry, and placed right in the middle of Scripture as if God wanted to make sure you couldn't miss them.

Those two books are Song of Songs and Lamentations.

On the surface, they couldn't be more different. Song of Songs is a love poem. It's passionate, joyful, and sometimes so intimate that readers throughout history have blushed while reading it. Two people are falling in love, admiring each other, longing for each other, and celebrating the kind of relationship that makes the whole world feel alive. It is, without exaggeration, the most romantic thing in the Bible.

Lamentations is the opposite. It's a funeral song for a destroyed city. Jerusalem has been burned to the ground by the Babylonian army. The temple is rubble. The people are dead or dragged into exile. And the poet sits in the ashes and weeps—not quietly, but loudly, angrily, desperately, pouring out grief so raw that it's almost hard to read.

Love and grief. Celebration and devastation. A wedding and a funeral.

So why are we reading them together?

Because the Bible insists that both of these experiences belong to God. He is not only the God of Sunday mornings and answered prayers. He is the God of the sleepless night when your heart is breaking. He is the God who invented romance and who sits with you in the ruins. He is the God who says, "Love is as strong as death," and who also lets you scream at him when death seems to have won.

Song of Songs and Lamentations, taken together, tell us that the full range of human emotion has a place in our relationship with God. You don't have to filter yourself. You don't have to show up with only your good feelings and leave the rest at the door. The same Bible that celebrates the heights of love also gives voice to the lowest depths of grief, and it treats both with absolute honesty.

That matters. Especially when you're twelve years old and your emotions are bigger than they've ever been, and nobody seems to have told you that God is okay with all of it.

WHAT YOU'RE ABOUT TO READ

The first half of this book covers Song of Songs. Don't let the name confuse you. "Song of Songs" is a way of saying "the greatest song ever written." It's a collection of love poems between a young man and a young woman, and it deals with themes you might not expect to find in Scripture: desire, beauty, jealousy, patience, and the power of committed love.

Some of it might make you uncomfortable. That's okay. Song of Songs doesn't pretend that love is a neat, sanitized, G-rated experience. It's honest about the fact that love is powerful, and powerful things demand respect. One of the book's most important refrains, repeated three times, is a warning: "Do not awaken love until the time is right." That message was written thousands of years ago, but it might be the most relevant thing anyone could say to your generation right now.

Chapter One walks you through the opening poems of the Song, where two people begin to express their feelings for each other and we learn that real love sees past insecurity to find genuine beauty.

Chapter Two follows their relationship through courtship to commitment, showing the contrast between love that is real and love that is only a show.

Chapter Three takes an honest look at what happens when love grows careless and comfortable, and how grace and friendship can rebuild what neglect has broken.

Chapter Four brings us to the climax of the entire Song, the declaration that love is "as strong as death" and burns with the very flame of God.

The second half of this book covers Lamentations. If the Song of Songs is the Bible's wedding, Lamentations is its funeral.

Lamentations was written in the aftermath of the worst disaster in Israel's history. In 586 BC, the Babylonian army destroyed Jerusalem, burned the temple, and carried the survivors into exile. The poet who wrote these five poems was not writing from a safe distance. He was sitting in the rubble. And he did something extraordinary: instead of offering explanations or theological lectures, he grieved. Loudly. Honestly. Angrily. He brought every raw, unfiltered emotion to God and laid it on the page.

Chapter Five introduces you to the grieving city, personified as a woman sitting alone in the dark, weeping with no one to comfort her.

Chapter Six turns the spotlight on God and asks the hardest question in the book: what do you do when the one who is supposed to protect you seems to be the one who destroyed you?

Chapter Seven takes us to the theological heart of Lamentations, where a man who has lost everything suddenly remembers something that changes his perspective forever: "His mercies are new every morning. Great is your faithfulness."

Chapter Eight walks through the final two poems, where the people pick up the pieces of their shattered world and offer a prayer that still echoes today: "Restore us to yourself, Lord, and we will be restored."

BEFORE WE BEGIN

Song of Songs is love poetry, and some of it is mature. The book celebrates romantic love between a man and a woman, and it doesn't always use tame language to do it. We're going to handle this honestly but carefully. You'll understand what the book is saying and why it matters without needing a commentary to decode every image. The Bible is not embarrassed by love, and neither should we be. But the Bible also takes love seriously, and that's the tone we'll follow.

Lamentations is grief poetry, and some of it is devastating. It describes famine, violence, destruction, and suffering in terms that are meant to make you feel something. The poet isn't trying to give you information. He's trying to make you understand what it was like. Some of it will be hard to read. That's by design. Grief that doesn't cost you anything isn't really grief.

Both books are poetry. That means they work differently from narrative books like Exodus or Judges. Poetry uses images, metaphors, and repetition to communicate. The man in Song of Songs doesn't literally think his beloved's hair looks like a herd of goats. The woman in Lamentations isn't literally a widow. But the images are powerful precisely because they are unexpected. Let them do their work. Don't rush past them looking for the "point." Often the image is the point.

And both books point to Jesus. Song of Songs shows us a love so fierce that it cannot be conquered by death, a love that burns with the flame of God himself. That kind of love found its ultimate expression on the cross, where Jesus loved his people with a commitment that not even the grave could break.

Lamentations shows us a people who have lost everything and cry out, "Restore us to yourself!" That prayer was answered when God entered the ruins of the human condition in the person of his Son, not to explain suffering from a distance but to share it, and then to conquer it.

These are two of the rawest books in the Bible. One celebrates what every human heart longs for. The other voices what every human heart fears. Together, they tell us that God meets us in both places, in the joy and in the grief, in the singing and in the silence.

Ready? Let's begin.

Turn the page.

1

THE GREATEST LOVE SONG EVER WRITTEN

Have you ever watched a movie where two characters obviously like each other, but neither one will say it? Maybe you've seen *Pride and Prejudice*, either the movie or the book by Jane Austen. Elizabeth Bennet and Mr. Darcy spend most of the story misunderstanding each other, misjudging each other, and driving each other crazy. She thinks he's arrogant. He thinks she's beneath him. And yet underneath all that friction, something is building. You can feel it. Every awkward conversation, every stolen glance, every argument that gets a little too personal. The audience knows what's coming long before Elizabeth and Darcy do.

And when Darcy finally writes that letter, when he finally lays his heart bare and tells her the truth about who he is, everything shifts. Elizabeth starts to see him differently. She realizes she was wrong. And slowly, carefully, the walls between them come down.

That moment when someone finally says what they really feel—when they stop hiding behind pride or fear or distance—is one of the most powerful things in all of storytelling. We never get tired of it. Whether it's a novel written two hundred years ago or a movie that came out last summer, a good love story grabs us because deep down, we all want to be known and loved by someone who sees us for who we really are.

The Song of Songs is that kind of story. Except it's not a novel or a movie. It's a poem. Actually, it's a collection of poems, and they are some of the most beautiful and surprising words in the entire Bible. The Song of Songs is a love story between a young man and a young woman, told almost entirely through their own voices. They speak to each other, about each other, and sometimes past each other, the way people do when they're falling in love.

And here's what might surprise you: the Bible isn't embarrassed by any of it.

WHAT IS THE SONG OF SONGS?

The title "Song of Songs" is a Hebrew way of saying "the greatest song." It's the same kind of phrase as "King of Kings" or "Holy of Holies." Whoever gave this book its title believed it was the most sublime song ever written. And what is this greatest of all songs about?

Love. Real, honest, heart-pounding love between a man and a woman.

If that surprises you, you're not alone. A lot of people are shocked to find out that the Bible contains love poetry. Some of it is pretty intense. For centuries, readers have debated what to do with this book. Some people have tried to make it purely symbolic, arguing that it's *only* about God's love for his people and has nothing to do with actual romance. Others have swung the other direction and treated it like an ancient dating manual.

The truth is somewhere in between, and it's far more interesting than either extreme. The Song of Songs is a real celebration of real love between a real man and a real woman. But because human love at its best reflects something about God's love for his people, the Song also points beyond itself to a deeper story. We'll get to that. But first, we need to listen to what these two young lovers are actually saying.

A VOICE FULL OF LONGING

The Song opens not with a narrator or a setting or a "once upon a time." It opens with a young woman's voice, and she gets right to the point. She is thinking about the man she loves, and she isn't shy about saying so. She talks about wanting to be near him, about how his very name makes her heart race, about how his presence is better than the finest wine.

This is important. The woman speaks first in the Song of Songs. She speaks more often than the man does throughout the entire book. She is confident, expressive, and bold about her feelings. She is not sitting quietly in a corner waiting to be noticed. She knows what she wants, and she's not afraid to say it.

At the same time, she's not reckless. She longs for the man to take the lead. She wants him to come to her, to pursue her, to sweep her off her feet. There's a beautiful balance here. She is strong and self-assured, but she also wants to be cherished and sought after. Those two things aren't opposites. They go together.

Right from the start, the Song challenges some of the assumptions our culture makes about love. It's not about playing games or pretending you don't care. It's not about chasing someone who isn't interested. It's two people who genuinely admire each other, who are drawn to each other, and who aren't afraid to express it.

DARK BUT BEAUTIFUL

But the woman isn't all confidence. She has insecurities too, and she's honest about them.

She describes herself as "dark but beautiful." Now, this isn't about race or ethnicity. In her culture, having dark skin meant you worked outside in the sun. It meant you were poor. Wealthy women stayed indoors and kept their skin pale. This young woman had been forced to work in the vineyards by her brothers, and the harsh sun had darkened her complexion. She felt like she didn't measure up to the polished, put-together women of the city.

Sound familiar? Maybe you've never worked in a vineyard, but you probably know what it feels like to look at yourself and think, *I'm not enough.* Maybe you look at other kids at school who seem to have it all together and wonder why you can't be more like them. Maybe you worry about your appearance, your clothes, your family situation, things you can't control. That voice that whispers "you're not good enough" is one of the oldest lies in the world.

Here's what the man does when the woman shares her insecurities. He doesn't dismiss her feelings. He doesn't say, "Oh, stop worrying about it." Instead, he calls her "the most beautiful of women." He tells her she is stunning. He notices her and affirms her, right in the area where she feels most unlovely.

That's what real love does. It doesn't ignore your struggles. It sees you clearly, flaws and all, and says, "You are beautiful to me."

BACK AND FORTH

What follows in the rest of chapters 1–2 is a conversation between two people who are completely captivated by each other. They trade compliments back and forth. He compares her eyes to doves. She compares him to an apple tree whose shade she wants to rest under and whose fruit is sweet. He calls her a lily among thorns. She says he stands out among other men the way a fruit tree stands out in a wild forest.

Some of these comparisons sound a little unusual to us today. Nobody walks up to their crush and says, "You remind me of a really nice apple tree." But in the ancient world, these were vivid and meaningful images. When the woman said she wanted to sit in the man's shade, she was saying he made her feel safe and protected. When she said his fruit was sweet, she meant that everything he offered her was good. These weren't just pretty words. They were ways of saying, "I trust you. I admire you. I'm glad you're in my life."

And notice something crucial: they build each other up. Every word between them is affirming, encouraging, and kind. There's no manipulation here, no tearing each other down, no jealousy or possessiveness. This is what healthy love looks like, even at its earliest and most exciting stages.

SPRINGTIME AND WAITING

One of the most beautiful passages in the entire Song comes in chapter 2, when the man arrives like a gazelle leaping over the mountains. He's eager. He's excited. He peers through the window and calls out to the woman: "Come away with me! Winter is over. The rains have stopped. Flowers are blooming everywhere. You can hear the birds singing. The fig trees are budding and the grapevines are giving off their fragrance. Come away, my beautiful one!"

It's springtime. Everything in nature is waking up, bursting with life, practically shouting that the time for love has arrived.

But the woman says, "Not yet."

She doesn't reject him. She clearly loves him. She even says, "My beloved is mine and I am his." But she also recognizes that love is powerful, and powerful things need to be handled carefully. She mentions little foxes that can sneak into a vineyard and destroy the tender new blossoms. The vineyard is an image she uses throughout the Song for her own life, her own heart. And she knows that if love rushes ahead too fast, before the right time, even small threats can cause real damage.

Then she says something that she will repeat two more times before the Song is over, a refrain so important that it becomes one of the book's biggest themes: ***Do not awaken love until the time is right.***

That's not a rejection of love. It's a deep respect for love's power. She's saying that real love, the kind that lasts, is worth waiting for. Stirring it up too early—before the relationship is ready, before the commitment is in place—can ruin the very thing you're trying to build.

This is one of the most countercultural messages in the entire Bible. We live in a world that hates waiting. We want everything now. Instant downloads, fast food, immediate results.

The idea of waiting for something because it isn't ready yet feels almost ridiculous to us. But the Song says that when it comes to love, patience isn't weakness. It's wisdom.

WHAT THIS MEANS FOR US

So what does any of this have to do with you? You're twelve or fifteen or seventeen—not twenty-five. You're not picking out wedding invitations. But the Song of Songs has more to say to you right now than you might think.

First, you are more than your appearance. The woman in the Song felt insecure about how she looked. She worried that she didn't measure up. But the man who loved her saw her as the most beautiful woman in the world, not because she was perfect, but because she was *her*. You are going to face a thousand messages telling you that your worth depends on how you look, what you wear, how many followers you have, or how you compare to everyone else. Those messages are lies. Your value doesn't come from any of those things. It comes from the God who made you and calls you his own.

Second, words have incredible power. The man and the woman in the Song use their words to build each other up. They affirm, encourage, and celebrate each other. Think about how you use your words. Do you build people up or tear them down? A single kind word at the right moment can change someone's entire day. A cruel word can wound someone for years. The Song shows us that love speaks life into people.

Third, real love is worth waiting for. The woman's refrain, "Do not awaken love until the time is right," isn't just about romance. It's about learning to be patient with the things that matter most. Whether it's friendships, goals, or yes, eventually, romantic relationships, the best things in life can't be rushed. Trying to force something before it's ready almost always leads to disappointment. Wisdom means trusting that the right time will come.

Fourth, love at its best points to something bigger. The kind of love the Song describes, a love where two people truly see each other, truly cherish each other, truly commit to each other, is a reflection of the way God loves his people. The Bible tells us that God looks at his children and calls them beautiful, even when they feel broken and dark and not enough. He pursues us. He speaks life over us. He waits for us with patience we don't deserve. The Song of Songs is a love story between two people, but it echoes the greatest love story ever told, the story of a God who will stop at nothing to be with the people he loves.

TALKING POINTS

1. **The woman in the Song felt insecure about her appearance because she didn't match her culture's standard of beauty. Every culture has its own standards, and they change all the time.** What are some of the ways our culture today tells people they need to look or act in order to be "enough"? How can knowing that God made you on purpose help you push back against those messages?

2. **The man responded to the woman's insecurity not by brushing it off but by affirming her with specific, kind words. Think about someone in your life who might be feeling unseen or not good enough right now.** What could you say to them this week that would build them up?

3. **The Song says, "Do not awaken love until the time is right." This principle applies to more than just romance.** Can you think of a time when you rushed into something before you were ready, whether it was a friendship, a decision, or an opportunity? What happened? What would patience have looked like in that situation?

4. **The love described in the Song of Songs is mutual. Both people admire each other, respect each other, and use their words to encourage each other.** Why do you think it matters that love goes both directions? What's the difference between a relationship where both people build each other up and one where only one person does the giving?

5. **The Bible says that human love, at its best, reflects God's love for his people.** What are some ways that the love described in these first two chapters reminds you of how God treats us?

The Song of Songs is just getting started. The love between this man and this woman is about to be tested in ways neither of them expected.

Turn the page.

2

SEEKING AND FINDING

There's a scene near the end of *The Princess Bride* that might be the most famous wedding scene in movie history. The ancient clergyman stands before Prince Humperdinck and Buttercup and begins his long, slow speech: "Mawwiage. Mawwiage is what bwings us togevah today."

It's hilarious, of course. But if you step back and look at what's actually happening in that moment, it's heartbreaking. Buttercup doesn't love Prince Humperdinck. She loves Westley. The whole movie is about two people who are separated by impossible obstacles, who search for each other across oceans and through fire swamps and past rodents of unusual size, because their love is too strong to let anything keep them apart. Westley literally comes back from the dead for her. And now, in this wedding scene, Buttercup is about to marry the wrong person because she's given up hope that the right one will come. But Westley does come. At the last possible moment, true love wins.

What makes *The Princess Bride* work so well isn't just the comedy or the sword fights or the quotable lines. It's that underneath all of it, there's a simple and powerful idea: when love is real, you don't stop searching for the person you love. You fight through every obstacle. You refuse to give up. And in the end, that kind of love is more valuable than all the wealth and power in the world.

The section of Song of Songs we're looking at in this chapter is about exactly that. It's about searching and finding. It's about the difference between love that is real and love that is only a show. And at the center of it all, there's a wedding, not a comedy wedding with a funny clergyman, but a deeply intimate moment when two people who have waited and searched and longed for each other finally come together for good.

A DREAM IN THE DARK

Chapter 3 of the Song opens with the woman lying in bed at night, unable to sleep. She's alone, and she's aching for the man she loves. Remember, at the end of chapter 2 she had sent him away, wisely recognizing that the time wasn't right yet. She told him to wait. She was right to do that.

But wisdom doesn't make the waiting easy.

Night after night, she searches for him in her dreams. "I looked for the one my heart loves," she says. "I looked for him but did not find him." So in her dream, she gets up. She goes out into the city streets. She wanders through the squares and alleyways, desperately searching for him. For a young woman alone at night in an ancient city, this would have been dangerous. She didn't care. Her love was stronger than her fear.

She ran into the city watchmen, the men who patrolled the streets at night. "Have you seen the one my heart loves?" she asked them. They hadn't.

Three times she searched. Three times she came up empty. And then, almost immediately after she passed the watchmen, she found him. Just like that. She grabbed hold of him and wouldn't let go. She brought him back to a safe place, to the house where her mother lived, the place that meant security and home to her.

This dream tells us something important about love: it requires seeking. The woman didn't just lie in bed wishing things were different. She got up and went looking. She took risks. She asked for help. She refused to give up even after repeated disappointments.

And notice the pattern: she didn't find him where she expected. Not at home in bed. Not in the streets. Not through the watchmen, who were supposed to know everything going on in the city. She found him only after she had exhausted every other option, right around the next corner, when she least expected it.

If that sounds like how God works sometimes, it's because it is. The Bible is full of people who searched and waited and struggled before they found what they were looking for. Abraham waited decades for the son God promised. Joseph spent years in prison before God's plan became clear. The Israelites wandered forty years in the wilderness before reaching the Promised Land. Waiting and searching are not signs that something has gone wrong. They're often the very path God uses to bring us to the right place at the right time.

After she finds him, the woman repeats her refrain from the previous chapter: "Do not awaken love until the time is right." Even in the joy of finding him, she remembers the lesson. Love is powerful. Love is worth searching for. But love must not be rushed.

TWO KINDS OF LOVE

What comes next is one of the most surprising contrasts in the entire book. The scene shifts suddenly to a grand procession. Something magnificent is coming up from the wilderness, surrounded by clouds of perfume and incense. Sixty of Israel's mightiest warriors march alongside it, every one of them armed with a sword. And at the center of it all is Solomon, the king, reclining on a spectacular royal bed made of the finest wood from Lebanon, with silver posts, a golden canopy, and purple cushions.

It sounds impressive. It sounds like the kind of thing you'd want to see.

But the Song is not impressed.

To understand why, you need to know something about Solomon. Yes, he was the wisest king Israel ever had. Yes, he built the temple. But Solomon also had a spectacular failure. The Bible tells us that he had seven hundred wives and three hundred concubines (1 Kings 11:3). That's a thousand women, and the text makes it clear that many of these marriages were political arrangements, not love stories. Solomon collected wives the way some people collect trading cards. His relationships weren't built on the kind of searching, longing, personal love that the woman in the Song describes. They were built on power, wealth, and status.

So when the Song pauses to describe Solomon's grand procession, with its armed guards and its luxury and its spectacle, it's setting up a contrast. On one side, you have Solomon: rich, powerful, surrounded by splendor, but ultimately alone in any way that matters. His bed is magnificent, but there's no intimacy in it. His weddings are events, but they aren't love stories.

On the other side, you have the man and the woman in the Song. Their love isn't flashy. They don't have silver and gold. Their "bed" is the green grass under cedar trees (remember chapter 1?). But what they have is real. It's personal. It's mutual. They know each other, search for each other, wait for each other.

The Song is saying something bold here: all the wealth and power in the world cannot create what these two ordinary people have. A thousand political marriages aren't worth one genuine love story. The biggest, most impressive wedding procession in history is empty if the love at the center of it isn't real.

That's a message worth hearing, especially in a world that tells you success is about having more, looking better, and impressing everyone around you. The Song says the opposite. The richest life is the one built on genuine, faithful love, even if it looks ordinary from the outside.

YOU ARE BEAUTIFUL

After the contrast with Solomon, the man turns his full attention to the woman. And what follows is one of the most tender and detailed expressions of admiration in all of ancient literature.

He describes her beauty from head to toe. Her eyes are like doves behind her veil. Her hair flows like a flock of goats streaming down a mountainside (which sounds strange to us, but picture the shimmering movement of dark animals cascading down a green hill, and it starts to make sense). Her teeth are white and perfectly matched. Her lips are lovely. She carries herself with confidence and dignity.

Now, some of this poetry might make you giggle. Comparing someone's hair to goats and their teeth to sheep is not exactly how we'd write a love letter today. But here's what matters: the man sees her. He notices every detail. He takes the time to tell her, specifically and carefully, exactly what he finds beautiful about her.

Remember from chapter 1 that this woman felt insecure about her appearance. She thought she was too dark, too weather-beaten, too ordinary. And here is the man, looking at her with total attention and saying, in effect, "Let me tell you what I see when I look at you. Let me describe, piece by piece, how beautiful you are to me."

This isn't flattery. It's not manipulation. It's what love does. Love pays attention. Love notices the details. Love tells the truth about what it sees, and what it sees is beauty.

One more thing worth noticing: he begins with her eyes. Not with any other part of her body, but with her eyes, the most personal, most communicative feature a person has. When you look into someone's eyes, you're encountering *them*, not just their appearance. The man starts there because this isn't just physical attraction. He sees *her*.

THE LOCKED GARDEN

As the poem builds toward its climax, the man describes the woman using a new image: a garden. But not just any garden. A locked garden. A sealed fountain.

In the ancient world, wealthy people created private gardens surrounded by walls, filled with fruit trees, fragrant flowers, and flowing water. These gardens were exclusive. You couldn't just wander in off the street. They were places of beauty and abundance, reserved for those who had been invited in.

The man is saying that everything about this woman is precious, protected, and worth waiting for. She has guarded herself. She hasn't given herself away carelessly. Her garden is locked, and that locked gate is not a rejection. It's a sign of incredible value.

This image ties directly back to the "do not awaken love" refrain. Throughout the Song, the woman has been wise about timing. She sent the man away when it wasn't the right moment. She warned the daughters of Jerusalem not to rush into love. She understood that what she had to offer was too valuable to be treated carelessly.

And now, at last, the right time has come.

THE GARDEN OPENS

The turning point happens at the very end of chapter 4. The woman speaks. She invites the winds to blow through her garden and carry its fragrance to the man she loves. And then she says the words they've both been waiting for: "Come into your garden and taste its finest fruits."

The man responds immediately. He enters the garden. He celebrates. He uses eight different words for "my" and "mine" in a single verse, emphasizing that this relationship is now fully and exclusively theirs. She is his garden. He is her beloved. What was locked is now open. What was sealed is now flowing freely.

And then something remarkable happens. A voice speaks, one that doesn't belong to either the man or the woman. Some scholars think it's the voice of the community. Others think it might even be the voice of God himself. Whoever it is, the message is clear: this union—this marriage—is celebrated. It is good. "Eat, friends, and drink! Be intoxicated with love!"

This moment, right at the center of the entire book, is the Song's answer to the question, "What is love for?" Love is for this. For two people who have searched for each other, waited for each other, and committed themselves to each other, finally coming together in the security of a lifelong promise. The Song places this celebration of married love at the exact midpoint of the book, with equal numbers of lines before and after it, as if to say: this is the heart of everything.

The Bible is not embarrassed by this. God created love. God created marriage. God designed the kind of intimacy that the Song celebrates. And when that intimacy happens in the right way, at the right time, between two people who have made a covenant to each other, even heaven celebrates.

WHAT THIS MEANS FOR US

First, keep searching for what matters most. The woman didn't give up when she couldn't find the man right away. She kept looking, kept asking, kept pressing forward. In your own life, the things that matter most will rarely fall into your lap. Good friendships take effort. A strong relationship with God takes pursuit. Don't settle for what's easy when something better is worth the search.

Second, real love doesn't need to impress anyone. The contrast between Solomon's spectacular procession and the simple, genuine love between the man and the woman is one of the most important lessons in the Song. Our culture constantly tells you that more is better, that bigger is better, that flashy and expensive equals valuable. But the Song says the quietest, most personal love is worth more than all the gold and armies in the world. Don't measure your relationships by how they look to other people. Measure them by whether they're real.

Third, what you protect becomes more valuable, not less. The locked garden isn't a negative image. It's a picture of something precious that has been cared for and guarded. When you protect your heart, your integrity, and your commitments, you aren't missing out. You're investing. The things you guard most carefully are the things that will mean the most when the right time comes to share them.

Fourth, God celebrates love done right. That mysterious voice at the end of this section, saying, "Eat, friends, and drink!" is a reminder that God is not a killjoy. He didn't create rules about love because he wants you to be miserable. He created boundaries because he wants you to experience something so good, so rich, so full that even heaven throws a party when it happens. God is for your joy, not against it.

TALKING POINTS

1. **The woman searched for the man she loved and didn't find him right away. She had to keep looking through failure and disappointment before she finally found him.** Have you ever had to be persistent in pursuing something important to you, whether it was a friendship, a goal, or your faith? What kept you going when you wanted to give up?

2. **The Song contrasts Solomon's wealth and power with the simple, genuine love between the man and the woman.** Why do you think people are so tempted to believe that having more stuff or more status will make them happy? What are some examples you've seen of people who have a lot but still seem to be missing something important?

3. **The man takes time to describe specifically what he finds beautiful about the woman. He doesn't give vague compliments; he notices the details.** Why do you think specific encouragement means more to people than generic praise? How could you be more intentional about noticing and naming what's good about the people around you?

4. **The image of the "locked garden" describes something valuable that has been protected and cared for.** What are some things in your own life that are worth guarding carefully, whether it's your character, your closest friendships, or your faith? What does it look like to protect those things without shutting people out completely?

5. **A mysterious voice at the center of the Song celebrates the love between the man and the woman. The Bible makes it clear that God delights in love done right.** How does it change the way you think about God to know that he's not just making rules about relationships but actually wants to celebrate them with you?

Love has been found. The garden has been opened. The celebration has begun. But the story isn't over, because even the strongest love will face its hardest test.

Turn the page.

3

WHEN LOVE GROWS COLD

Have you ever taken someone for granted? Maybe it was your best friend. For months or even years, they were always there. They sat with you at lunch. They texted you first. They showed up when you needed them. And because they were always there, you stopped noticing. You started canceling plans without thinking twice. You forgot to text back. You got busy with other things and assumed they'd just keep waiting around.

Then one day, something shifted. Maybe they started sitting with someone else. Maybe they stopped reaching out. Maybe they said something like, "It feels like you don't really care anymore." And suddenly your stomach dropped, because you realized they were right. You did care. You cared a lot. But you'd gotten so comfortable that you forgot to show it. And now the distance between you felt enormous, and you didn't know how to close it.

That panicked feeling—the one where you realize you've let something precious slip through your fingers because you got lazy or distracted or comfortable—is one of the most universal human experiences there is. It happens in friendships.

It happens in families. And according to the Song of Songs, it happens in love too.

The section we're about to look at is the most dramatic and emotionally raw part of the entire book. If the last chapter ended with a celebration, this chapter begins with a crisis. The couple who searched for each other, waited for each other, and finally came together in joyful commitment are about to discover that love doesn't stay alive on autopilot. Even the strongest relationship can grow cold if you stop paying attention.

But here's the good news: this chapter doesn't end in the cold. It ends with one of the most powerful reunions in all of Scripture.

A KNOCK AT THE DOOR

The trouble begins with a knock. The woman is in bed, half-asleep. It's nighttime. Her beloved comes to the door and calls out to her, piling up every affectionate name he has for her. He's been out in the cold, and his hair is wet with dew. He wants to come in. He wants to be with her.

And she says no.

Not a dramatic, angry no. Something worse. A lazy, indifferent no. "I've already gotten undressed," she says. "I've already washed my feet. Do I really have to get up?"

If you're reading that and thinking, *Wait, is this the same woman who couldn't sleep because she missed him so much? The one who braved the city streets at night just to find him?* then you're feeling exactly what the Song wants you to feel. This is the same woman. But something has changed. The urgency is gone. The desperation to be near him has faded into comfortable routine. She's warm. She's cozy. And getting out of bed to open the door feels like too much effort.

It's a painfully honest picture of what happens when we get comfortable in a relationship. The very closeness that love creates can become the thing that makes us careless. When someone is always there, it's easy to assume they always will be, no matter how little effort you put in.

The man tries one more time to reach her, stretching his hand through the opening in the door. And something finally stirs inside her. Her heart starts racing. She realizes what she's doing. She gets up, her hands trembling, and goes to open the door.

But he's gone.

SEARCHING IN THE DARK

The woman is devastated. She says her very soul left her body when she realized he had turned away. Now the roles are reversed. In chapter 3, she searched for him because she missed him. Here, she searches for him because she drove him away. The ache is sharper this time because she knows it's her own fault.

She goes out into the city, calling for him, looking everywhere. But unlike the earlier dream where the search ended quickly and safely, this time things go badly. The city watchmen find her wandering the streets at night, and instead of helping her, they beat her. They strip her outer garment. They treat her like someone who doesn't belong.

This is a dream, not a news report. The Song isn't giving us a literal account of what happened on a Tuesday night. It's using the logic of dreams to express something emotionally true: when you let love grow cold through carelessness, the consequences can be painful and disorienting. The world that once felt safe and welcoming starts to feel hostile. The distance between you and the person you love turns into something that hurts.

The woman doesn't give up, though. She turns to the daughters of Jerusalem, her circle of friends, and begs for their help. "If you find him," she says, "tell him I am sick with love."

And then the friends ask a question that changes everything.

WHAT MAKES HIM SO SPECIAL?

"What is your beloved more than any other?" the daughters of Jerusalem ask. "Why should we help you find him? What makes him so special?"

It's a simple question. But it forces the woman to stop, think, and remember. Instead of spiraling further into panic and guilt, she has to put into words exactly what it is about this man that makes him worth chasing through the dark.

And she rises to the occasion. What follows is the only place in the entire Song of Songs where the woman gives a full, detailed description of the man's appearance. She starts at the top and works her way down, and every image is full of admiration.

His appearance is radiant and healthy. His head is like the finest gold. His hair is dark as a raven. His eyes are gentle, like doves beside streams of water. His cheeks are fragrant, like beds of spices. His lips are soft, like lilies. His arms are strong, like rods of gold. His legs are like marble pillars set in sockets of gold. His overall presence is majestic, like the cedars of Lebanon, the tallest and most impressive trees in the ancient world.

And then she lands on the word that matters most. After describing his entire appearance, she comes back to his mouth, to his words, to his voice. "Everything about him is desirable," she says. "This is my beloved. This is my friend."

That last word is easy to miss, but it might be the most important word in her entire speech. After all the romantic poetry, after all the imagery of gardens and springtime and gazelles, she calls him her *friend*. Not just her lover. Not just the man who makes her heart race. Her friend. The person she actually likes being around. The person she trusts. The person whose company she enjoys even when the fireworks aren't going off.

The Song is quietly making a profound point: the deepest romantic love is built on genuine friendship. Physical attraction fades and flickers. Excitement comes and goes. But friendship, real friendship, is the foundation that holds everything together when the feelings aren't cooperating.

FOUND AGAIN

After hearing the woman's passionate description, the daughters of Jerusalem offer to help search. But something has already shifted. The act of describing him, of remembering who he is and why she loves him, has unlocked something in the woman's heart. She doesn't need the search party anymore. She suddenly knows exactly where he is.

"He has gone down to his garden," she says. "He is gathering lilies."

The garden. Their garden. The same garden from chapter 4, the place that represents their love, their intimacy, their shared life. He hasn't abandoned her. He hasn't left for good. He's right where he's always been, tending the relationship, waiting for her to come back.

And then she says the refrain that has echoed through the entire Song, but this time it sounds different. It sounds like coming home after being lost. "I am my beloved's, and my beloved is mine."

The crisis is over. Not because the problem wasn't real, but because the woman did the hard work of remembering, pursuing, and returning. She didn't let her guilt paralyze her. She didn't let her failure define the relationship. She went looking for him, and she found him still faithful, still present, still hers.

AS BEAUTIFUL AS THE DAY I MARRIED YOU

What the man says next is extraordinary. After being shut out, after being rejected on a cold night, after watching her let their love grow lazy, he doesn't punish her. He doesn't give her the silent treatment. He doesn't list all the ways she let him down.

He tells her she's beautiful.

He uses almost exactly the same words he used on their wedding day. Her eyes are still doves. Her hair still flows like a flock of dark goats streaming down a hillside. Her teeth are still white and perfectly matched. Her face is still lovely behind her veil.

That detail about the veil is significant. Veils were associated with weddings in the ancient world. By mentioning the veil, the man is reaching all the way back to the beginning. He's saying, in effect, "You are as beautiful to me right now as you were the day we stood together and made our promises. Nothing has changed. My love for you has not moved."

He goes even further. He compares her to beautiful cities, to the dawn breaking over the horizon, to the moon and the sun. He says she is unique among all women, that even queens and royal women would look at her and call her blessed. The very people she once felt inferior to, the sophisticated daughters of Jerusalem, now marvel at her.

This is what grace looks like inside a relationship. The man had every right to be hurt. He was hurt. But instead of wielding that hurt like a weapon, he used his words to rebuild. He reminded her of who she was. He reminded her of who they were together. He answered her failure not with punishment but with renewed commitment.

WHAT THIS MEANS FOR US

First, love requires attention, not just affection. The woman loved the man. That was never in question. But love that doesn't show up, love that can't be bothered to get out of bed, love that assumes the other person will always just be there, eventually creates distance. This is true in every relationship. Your friendships need tending. Your family relationships need effort. Your relationship with God needs pursuit. Feeling love isn't enough. You have to act on it.

Second, when you mess up, pursue, don't hide. The woman's first instinct after realizing her mistake was to go find him. She didn't sit in bed feeling sorry for herself. She didn't wait for him to come back and apologize (he hadn't done anything wrong). She got up and went looking. When you've hurt someone or let a relationship slip, the worst thing you can do is nothing. Go to them. Admit what happened. Do the work of repair.

Third, remembering why you love someone can pull you through a crisis. When the daughters of Jerusalem asked, "What's so special about him?" the woman had to articulate what she already knew in her heart. That act of remembering and speaking out loud what she valued about him was the turning point. When a relationship is struggling, it helps to stop and deliberately recall what drew you together in the first place. Gratitude is one of the most powerful forces in any relationship.

Fourth, grace rebuilds what carelessness breaks. The man's response to the woman's failure is one of the most beautiful pictures of grace in the Bible. He didn't hold a grudge. He didn't make her earn her way back. He met her with the same words of love he'd spoken from the very beginning. That's how God treats us too. When we wander, when we grow cold, when we can't be bothered to open the door, he doesn't stop loving us. He speaks the same words over us that he spoke at the beginning: "You are mine. You are beautiful. I haven't changed my mind about you."

TALKING POINTS

1. **The woman turned the man away not out of anger but out of laziness and comfort.** Why do you think it's sometimes harder to fight against indifference than against outright conflict? Can you think of a relationship in your life that you might be neglecting simply because you've gotten used to the other person always being there?

2. **When the daughters of Jerusalem asked, "What makes your beloved so special?" the woman had to put her feelings into words.** Why do you think it matters to actually say out

loud what you appreciate about someone? How might doing that regularly change your friendships or family relationships?

3. **The woman called the man both her beloved and her friend.** Why do you think friendship is such an important part of any deep relationship? What qualities make someone a truly great friend, and how are those qualities different from (or similar to) what makes someone fun to be around?

4. **The man responded to the woman's failure by telling her she was as beautiful as the day he married her. That's a picture of grace.** Have you ever had someone respond to your mistake with kindness instead of anger? How did that make you feel, and how did it affect the relationship going forward?

5. **The Bible teaches that God responds to us the way the man responded to the woman: with patience, grace, and a love that doesn't change based on our performance.** Why is it sometimes hard to believe that God's love for you doesn't depend on how well you're doing? What would it look like to really trust that?

The crisis has passed. Love has been tested and proven stronger than failure. But the Song isn't finished yet. There's still one more thing these two have to say about what love really is, and it might be the most important line in the entire book.

Turn the page.

4

LOVE STRONG AS DEATH

If you've ever read *Charlotte's Web* or seen the 1973 film, you know how the story ends. And if you're like most people, you cried.

Charlotte is a small gray spider who lives in the corner of a barn doorway. Wilbur is a pig who has been marked for slaughter. They have no business being friends. A spider and a pig don't exactly run in the same circles. But Charlotte decides that Wilbur's life matters, and she sets out to save him.

She does it with words. She weaves messages into her web, "Some Pig," "Terrific," "Radiant," "Humble," and those words change the way everyone sees Wilbur. The farmer who was going to kill him suddenly sees something valuable. The whole county shows up to marvel. Wilbur is saved.

But there's a cost. Charlotte pours her remaining strength into her final masterpiece, an egg sac that holds the next generation of her children. She knows she won't live to see them hatch. When Wilbur finds her after the fair, weak and fading, she tells him she won't be coming home. "Why did you do all this for me?" Wilbur asks. "I don't deserve any of it." Charlotte's answer is simple: "You have been my friend. That in itself is a tremendous thing."

Charlotte gives everything she has. Not because Wilbur earned it. Not because she'll get something in return. She gives her life freely, without conditions, because that's what love does.

Every time I watch that scene, I think of the Song of Songs. Because right here, at the climax of the Bible's great love poem, the woman says something that people have been quoting for three thousand years:

"Love is as strong as death."

That single line is the summit of everything the Song has been building toward. Every longing glance, every midnight search, every season of waiting, every failure and reunion has been leading to this one declaration. Charlotte's story is beautiful because it illustrates a shadow of this truth: love that is real will give everything, even life itself, for the beloved. And what the woman says about love in these final chapters isn't just poetry. It's one of the boldest theological claims in the entire Bible.

THE WHOLE PERSON

As the Song moves into its final stretch, the man speaks one more time about the woman's beauty. This time his description starts not with her eyes (as it did earlier) but with her feet and moves upward, taking in her whole body. His admiration is total and unashamed. He compares her graceful movements to a dancer, her figure to a palm tree, her presence to something so captivating that he can barely contain himself.

What's striking here isn't just the poetry. It's the fact that this comes *after* the crisis of chapter 5, after the night when she turned him away, after the painful search and the tearful reunion. He isn't describing a woman he's just met. He's describing a woman he's fought with, forgiven, and chosen again. His admiration isn't the breathless infatuation of a first date. It's the deeper appreciation of someone who has been through difficulty and come out the other side still committed.

The woman responds with words that echo one of the Song's most important refrains, but with a subtle change. Earlier she said, "My beloved is mine, and I am his." Now she says, "I am my beloved's, and his desire is for me." Did you catch the shift? The first version put herself first: *my* beloved is *mine*. This version puts him first: *I am his*. It's a small change, but it reflects growth. She's moved from the excitement of new love, where you can't believe this amazing person wants to be with *you*, to the security of mature love, where you rest in belonging to each other.

She invites him to come away with her to the countryside, to the vineyards and fields where they can enjoy each other away from the pressures of daily life. She mentions mandrakes and pomegranates, images associated with fruitfulness and new life. She's not just thinking about right now. She's thinking about the future, about the family they'll build, about the life that will grow from their love.

THE FINAL WARNING

Before the Song reaches its great climax, the woman pauses for one last time to repeat her refrain to the daughters of Jerusalem: "Do not awaken love until the time is right."

This is the third and final time she says it. She's said it after moments of desire, after moments of joy, and now after the full experience of love's highs and lows. She knows what she's talking about. She has lived through the waiting, the wedding, the crisis, and the reunion. And her conclusion, after all of it, is the same message she gave at the very beginning: love is powerful, and powerful things demand respect. Don't rush it. Don't treat it carelessly. The fact that love is beautiful doesn't mean love is safe.

It's the kind of warning that only someone with experience can give. A child who has never touched a hot stove can be told that the burner is dangerous. But the warning means something different coming from someone who has been burned. The woman has tasted love's sweetness and felt love's sting. Her warning isn't theory. It's testimony.

THE STRONGEST FORCE IN THE WORLD

And now we arrive at the peak. The woman asks her beloved to place her like a seal over his heart, like a seal on his arm. In the ancient world, a seal was one of the most personal things a person could own. It was used to sign documents, mark property, and prove identity. You carried your seal everywhere. You never let it out of your sight. When the woman asks to be his seal, she's asking for permanence. She's saying, "Carry me with you always. Let me be as close to you as your own heartbeat, as inseparable from you as your own arm."

And then she explains why: "Love is as strong as death. Its jealousy is as enduring as the grave. It burns like a blazing fire, like a mighty flame. Many waters cannot quench love; rivers cannot sweep it away. If a man offered all the wealth of his house for love, he would be utterly scorned."

Read that again slowly.

Love is as strong as death. Think about what that means. Death is the most powerful force any human being ever encounters. It is final. It is unstoppable. Every person who has ever lived has fallen under its grip. And the woman says love matches it. Love grips you and won't let go, the same way death grips and won't let go. Love is relentless, unyielding, fierce. It cannot be reasoned with or bargained away or diluted.

Its jealousy is as enduring as the grave. This isn't the petty jealousy of someone who gets upset because you talked to another person at a party. This is the fierce, exclusive commitment that says, "You are mine and I am yours, and nothing in the world will change that." The grave doesn't share. It doesn't take half measures. And neither does real love.

It burns like a mighty flame. Some translations say this flame is "the very flame of the Lord." If that's the right reading, then the Song is saying that the fire of love comes from God himself. Love isn't just a human feeling. It has a divine origin. The same God who spoke galaxies into existence also kindled the fire of love in the human heart.

Many waters cannot quench it. Rivers cannot wash it away. This is the language of Noah's flood, of the Red Sea, of every overwhelming catastrophe in the Bible. The Song is saying that you can throw everything at love—every disaster, every heartbreak, every failure, every year of distance and difficulty—and it will still be burning when the floodwaters recede.

And finally: *love cannot be bought.* If someone offered

everything they owned in exchange for love, they would be laughed at. You can't purchase it. You can't earn it. You can't manufacture it with money or power or status. This is the Song's last word about Solomon and his thousand wives. All his wealth couldn't buy what this ordinary couple has for free.

THE WOMAN STANDS HER GROUND

After this extraordinary declaration, the Song flashes back to an earlier time. The woman's brothers appear, talking about her as if she's not even in the room. They see her as a child, not yet old enough for marriage. They're already making plans to "improve" her so they can find a good match for her, someone who will pay a high bride price and benefit the family.

The woman interrupts them. "I am a wall," she says. "My breasts are like towers." In other words: I'm not a child anymore. I don't need you to dress me up or market me. God has given me everything I need.

But she doesn't just assert her independence. She says something even more significant: "I have become in his eyes like one who brings peace." That word for peace is connected to the word used earlier when the man called her his "Shulammite," his peaceful one, his complete one. She brings wholeness to her beloved not because her brothers packaged her attractively, but because she gave herself freely to the man of her choosing.

This is a powerful statement about what love is not. Love is not a business transaction. It's not an arrangement made over someone's head. It's not about maximizing value or finding the highest bidder. Love is a free gift between two people who choose each other, and no amount of scheming by well-meaning (or not-so-well-meaning) family members can manufacture it.

The Song reinforces this with one final contrast between Solomon and the couple. Solomon had a vast vineyard at a place whose name means "lord of the multitude." He managed his vineyard through hired keepers and collected a fortune in silver from it. The woman says: my vineyard is my own. It isn't leased out. It isn't managed by someone else. It belongs to me, and I give it to who I choose.

THE SONG THAT NEVER ENDS

The final verses of the Song are brief and beautiful. The man asks to hear her voice one more time. The woman responds by telling him to come to her like a gazelle on the mountains of spices, the same image from the very beginning of the book. It's as if the Song has come full circle. The longing that opened the poem is still alive. The desire hasn't faded. The love that began in chapter 1 is still burning at the end of chapter 8.

And that's the point. The Song doesn't end with a neat conclusion. It ends with an invitation. Come back. Come closer. Let me hear your voice again. Love isn't a destination you arrive at and unpack your bags. It's a living, breathing, ongoing relationship that keeps calling you forward, keeps drawing you in, keeps asking for more of you.

The Song of Songs is the Bible's way of saying: this is what love was always meant to be. Not a transaction. Not a conquest. Not a temporary thrill. But a fire that burns with the very flame of God, a force as relentless as death, a commitment that no flood can drown and no fortune can buy.

WHAT THIS MEANS FOR US

First, the strongest things in the world aren't physical. Death seems like the ultimate power. Money seems like it can buy anything. But the Song says love is stronger than death and more valuable than all the wealth in the world. When you're deciding what to invest your life in, remember that. Careers end. Bank accounts empty. But the love you build with the people around you, and the love God has for you, will outlast everything.

Second, love is not for sale. This is the Song's final word on Solomon: all his wealth and all his wives couldn't produce what the man and woman have. Our culture constantly tells you that more is better, that you can buy happiness if you just get the right thing. The Song laughs at that idea. The most valuable things in life, genuine love, real friendship, faithful commitment, can never be purchased. They can only be given freely.

Third, your story is yours. The woman's brothers tried to control her future, to decide her worth for her. She refused. She knew her own value and made her own choice. You're going to face pressure from all kinds of sources telling you who to be, what to want, and how to measure your worth. Don't let anyone else write your story for you. You are not a product to be marketed. You are a person made in the image of God, with a life and a future that belong to him and to you.

Fourth, God's love is the fire behind every good love. If the "mighty flame" of Song 8:6 really is "the flame of the Lord," then every act of genuine love in your life is a spark from the heart of God. Every time someone forgives you, stays with you, fights for you, or refuses to give up on you, you're getting a glimpse of the God who invented love in the first place.

And his love truly is stronger than death. The cross proved it. The empty tomb confirmed it. Nothing, not even the grave, can separate you from the love of God. The one who loves you most will love you beyond death and into eternity.

TALKING POINTS

1. **The woman says love is "as strong as death."** What do you think she means by that? In what ways is love similar to death in its power over people? How is love different from (and ultimately better than) death?

2. **The Song says that if someone tried to buy love with all the wealth of their house, they would be "utterly scorned."** Why do you think people still try to buy love or earn it, whether with money, popularity, or achievements? What does it look like to truly receive love as a free gift?

3. **The woman's brothers tried to control her future, but she stood up for herself and made her own choice.** Have you ever felt pressure from others to be someone you're not or to measure up to a standard that didn't fit you? How did you handle it, and what did you learn?

4. **The Song ends not with a conclusion but with an invitation: "Come back. Let me hear your voice."** Why do you think the poet chose to end the book this way instead of giving it a neat, tidy ending? What does that tell us about the nature of love?

5. **The Song suggests that the fire of love comes from God himself, that every genuine act of love is a spark from his heart.** If that's true, what does that say about the small, everyday acts of kindness and loyalty you experience in your

own life? How does it change the way you think about an encouraging word from a friend, a parent's sacrifice, or a stranger's unexpected generosity?

The Song of Songs has given us a vision of love at its most beautiful, most honest, and most powerful. A fire that burns with the flame of God. A force that death itself cannot conquer. But the Bible doesn't only speak about love's heights. It also speaks about love's depths, about what happens when everything you cherish is ripped away and all you have left is grief.

Turn the page.

5

THE CITY THAT SITS ALONE

If you've seen *The Land Before Time*, you probably remember the scene that changed everything. Littlefoot is a young dinosaur whose mother has just fought off a terrifying Sharptooth to save his life. She's badly hurt. Littlefoot finds her lying in the rain, barely able to speak. She tells him he has to find the Great Valley on his own now. She tells him she'll always be with him, even if he can't see her. And then she dies.

What follows is one of the most heartbreaking sequences in any animated film. Littlefoot wanders alone through a barren, ash-colored landscape. The world that was once green and full of life is now gray and empty. He sees his own shadow and, for a moment, thinks it's his mother. He calls out to her. But it's just a shadow, and he's just alone.

It's the kind of scene that stays with you long after the movie ends. Not because it's dramatic or exciting, but because it's honest. It shows you what grief actually feels like: the emptiness, the loneliness, the desperate wish that you could go back to the way things were. The whole world looks different when you've lost something you can never get back.

The book of Lamentations begins in exactly that place. Except it's not a young dinosaur mourning his mother. It's an entire city mourning everything.

A DIFFERENT KIND OF BOOK

Before we go any further, let's step back and talk about what Lamentations is and why it's in the Bible.

The Song of Songs gave us the highest heights of human emotion: love, desire, joy, celebration. Lamentations gives us the lowest depths: grief, loss, devastation, and the agonizing question of what to do when it seems like God himself has turned against you.

Lamentations was written in the aftermath of the worst disaster in ancient Israel's history. In 586 BC, the Babylonian army, led by King Nebuchadnezzar, besieged Jerusalem for eighteen months. The people inside the city walls slowly starved. When the walls finally fell, the Babylonians destroyed everything. They burned the temple, the palace, and the houses. They tore down the city walls. They killed many of the people and dragged most of the survivors away into exile in Babylon.

Try to imagine what that would feel like. The city where your family had lived for generations, gone. The temple where your parents and grandparents had worshiped God, a pile of rubble. Your friends and neighbors, either dead or marched away in chains. Everything that made your life feel stable and meaningful, erased.

That's the world Lamentations was written in. And the poet doesn't try to explain it away or rush past the pain. He sits in it. For five entire chapters, the book does nothing but grieve.

It is the Bible's way of saying: when your world falls apart, you are allowed to feel it. You are allowed to cry. You are allowed to be angry. You are allowed to bring every raw, ugly, honest emotion to God and pour it out at his feet.

One more thing you should know: Lamentations is written as an acrostic. In the original language, each verse of chapter 1 begins with the next letter of the Hebrew alphabet, from start to finish. All twenty-two letters, in order. That might seem like a strange thing to do in a poem about grief. Why would you impose such a strict structure on something so painful?

Think of it this way. When your emotions are completely overwhelming, when the pain is so big you don't even know where to start, sometimes having a structure is the only thing that keeps you from falling apart. The acrostic form is like a container for grief that would otherwise be too enormous to hold. It's the poet's way of saying: I will walk through this pain from A to Z, one letter at a time, and I will not skip a single step.

A WOMAN SITTING ALONE

Lamentations 1 opens with a single word that sets the tone for everything that follows. In the original language, the word is a cry of anguish, something like "Alas!" or "How!" It's the kind of sound you make when you see something so terrible that words almost fail you.

And then the poet does something remarkable. Instead of describing the city as a pile of broken stones and burned buildings, he describes it as a person. Jerusalem becomes a woman. She sits alone, weeping in the night, tears streaming down her face.

The contrast between what she was and what she has become is devastating. She was once full of people, now she sits alone. She was once great among the nations, now she is like a widow. She was once a princess, now she is a slave. Every line swings between the glory of the past and the misery of the present, like a pendulum that keeps hitting you in the chest.

The image of a widow is especially powerful. In the ancient world, a widow without sons had almost no one to protect or provide for her. She was among the most vulnerable people in society. By calling Jerusalem a widow, the poet is saying: this city that was once protected by God himself now sits exposed and defenseless. The husband who should have been watching over her seems to be gone.

And her children, the people who once filled her streets, are gone too. They've been dragged away into exile. The roads that used to be packed with pilgrims heading to the temple for worship are empty. The gates are deserted. The priests who used to lead joyful celebrations now groan in despair. The young women who used to sing at festivals now have nothing left to sing about.

NO ONE TO COMFORT HER

One phrase echoes through Lamentations 1 like a heartbeat: "There is no one to comfort her."

It appears again and again. No comforter among her former allies. No comforter among her friends. No comforter to stand beside her in her grief. The nations she had trusted as partners have betrayed her and become her enemies. The political alliances she relied on have evaporated. She is utterly, completely alone.

In ancient culture, when someone was grieving, friends and family were expected to come and sit with them, to share the burden of their sorrow. Think of how, when someone dies today, people bring food and send cards and show up at the house. Not because they can fix anything, but because being present with someone in their pain is one of the most important things a human being can do. Jerusalem has none of that. She grieves alone, and the loneliness makes the grief even worse.

If you've ever gone through something hard and felt like nobody understood, like nobody was coming to help, like you were carrying the weight entirely by yourself, then you know a fraction of what this chapter is describing.

WHY THIS HAPPENED

The poem doesn't hide the reason for Jerusalem's devastation. Woven into the grief is an honest confession: this happened because of sin.

The poet uses a word that means "rebellion" to describe what Jerusalem did. This wasn't one small mistake or an accidental slip. Israel had a covenant with God, a sacred agreement. God would be their protector, and they would be faithful to him. But over and over, for centuries, the people broke that covenant. They worshiped other gods. They ignored the poor and the vulnerable. They trusted foreign nations instead of trusting God. The prophets warned them again and again that this path would lead to disaster, and they refused to listen.

Now the disaster has arrived, and it looks exactly like what the prophets predicted. The curses spelled out in Deuteronomy 28, warnings given to Israel hundreds of years earlier, have come true. Your enemies will become your masters. Your children will be taken into captivity. You will find no resting place among the nations.

But here's what makes Lamentations so remarkable: the confession of sin doesn't cancel out the grief. The poet doesn't say, "Well, we deserved it, so we shouldn't be sad." He says, in effect, "We sinned, and God was right to punish us, and it is absolutely devastating, and we are going to cry about it." Both things are true at the same time. Responsibility and sorrow stand side by side. Lamentations refuses to let you choose between them.

IS THERE ANY SORROW LIKE MY SORROW?

Halfway through the chapter, something shifts. A new voice takes over. It's Jerusalem herself, the grieving woman, speaking directly.

She turns to the people passing by and cries out with words that have echoed down through the centuries: "Is there any sorrow like my sorrow?"

She isn't asking a statistical question. She isn't literally claiming that no one in history has ever suffered this much. She's doing what every grieving person does: trying to make someone understand the sheer weight of what she's carrying. When your pain is that deep, it feels like no one could possibly comprehend it. You need someone, anyone, to stop and look and acknowledge that what has happened to you is real and terrible.

Then she describes what God has done to her. Fire sent into her bones. A net spread for her feet. A yoke made from her own sins, placed on her neck until she collapsed under the weight. Young men crushed like grapes in a winepress. She weeps, and her tears flow like water, and still there is no one to comfort her.

The theological tension here is staggering. Jerusalem knows that God is behind her suffering. She says so plainly: "The Lord has brought this grief upon me." And yet she doesn't stop talking to him. She doesn't walk away from God. She turns toward him and says, "Look! See my pain!" She calls him Lord even while accusing him of devastating her.

This is one of the most important things the Bible teaches us about faith: honest grief and real trust are not opposites. You can be furious with God and still believe he's the only one who can help. You can accuse him of causing your pain and still cry out for his mercy. The people in the Bible who had the deepest relationships with God were often the ones who were most brutally honest with him. Think of Job. Think of David in the Psalms. Think of Jesus in the garden of Gethsemane, sweating blood and asking his Father to take the cup of suffering away.

Faith doesn't mean putting on a happy face and pretending everything is fine. Faith means bringing everything you have, including your anger, your confusion, your grief, and your doubt, and laying it at God's feet because you still believe he's listening, even when it doesn't feel like it.

WHAT THIS MEANS FOR US

First, grief is not the opposite of faith. Lamentations is in the Bible for a reason. God included an entire book of weeping, mourning, and raw complaint in his Word because he wants you to know that those emotions have a place in your relationship with him. If you're going through something painful, you don't have to pretend you're okay. Bring it to God. He can handle it.

Second, loneliness makes pain worse. The refrain "no one to comfort her" is a reminder that human beings need each other. When someone you know is hurting, one of the most powerful things you can do is simply be present. You don't have to have answers. You don't have to fix anything. Just show up. Sit with them. Let them know they aren't alone.

Third, sin has real consequences, but consequences don't erase compassion. Jerusalem's suffering was the result of centuries of rebellion against God. The poet acknowledges that honestly. But he doesn't use that fact to shut down sympathy. He still weeps for her. He still wants God to see her pain. When someone is suffering the consequences of their own choices, the right response isn't "Well, you brought this on yourself." The right response is compassion first, truth alongside it, and grace always.

Fourth, it's okay to say "this is the worst thing that has ever happened to me." Jerusalem's cry, "Is there any sorrow like my sorrow?" isn't self-pity. It's an honest expression of overwhelming pain. When you're in the middle of something terrible, you don't need someone telling you that other people have it worse. You need someone who will look at your pain and say, "I see it. It's real. And I'm not going anywhere."

TALKING POINTS

1. **Lamentations is structured as an acrostic, walking through the alphabet one letter at a time.** Why do you think the poet chose such a structured form for such an emotional

subject? Can you think of times in your own life when having a routine or structure helped you get through a difficult season?

2. **The repeated phrase "there is no one to comfort her" highlights Jerusalem's loneliness in grief.** Why do you think loneliness makes suffering so much harder? What can you do to be a comforter for someone in your life who might be going through a hard time?

3. **The poet acknowledges Jerusalem's sin and God's justice, but he also weeps over her pain and asks God to see her suffering.** How do you hold both things together, knowing that someone's pain is partly their own fault but still caring about them and wanting to help?

4. **Jerusalem cries out to God even though she believes God is the one who caused her suffering.** What does it tell us about the nature of faith that she keeps talking to God even in her anger and grief? Have you ever been angry with God? What did you do with that feeling?

5. **Lamentations shows us that the Bible makes room for raw, unfiltered grief.** How does knowing this change the way you think about bringing your honest emotions to God? Is there something you've been holding back from telling him because you thought it wasn't "okay" to feel that way?

Lamentations 1 gave Jerusalem a voice to cry out in her grief. But the poet isn't finished. The next chapter will turn the spotlight directly on God and ask the hardest question of all: what do you do when it seems like God himself is the one who destroyed you?

Turn the page.

6

THE DAY GOD'S ANGER BURNED

If you've seen the film *Hugo*, you know it's a story about a boy who lives in the walls of a Paris train station, winding the clocks and trying to fix a broken mechanical man his father left behind. But at the heart of the movie is a mystery: who is the bitter old man running the toy shop?

Hugo discovers that he is Georges Méliès, once the most imaginative filmmaker in the world. Méliès built astonishing things. He invented special effects. He created magical worlds on screen that nobody had ever seen before, worlds where rockets flew to the moon and magicians made people vanish and the impossible happened right before your eyes. He was a builder of wonders, an artist whose creations left audiences breathless.

And then he destroyed it all himself.

After the world moved on and stopped caring about his films, Méliès didn't just walk away from what he'd made. He burned his sets. He melted hundreds of his own films down into chemicals used for making boot heels. He buried every trace of his life's work as if it had never existed. The man who created the magic took it apart with his own hands. When

Hugo finds him, Méliès is a hollowed-out shell living among the ruins of his own legacy, and he doesn't want anyone to remind him of what he once built.

That image of a creator deliberately dismantling his own masterpiece is exactly what you'll find in Lamentations 2. If chapter 1 was a grieving woman sitting alone in the ruins, chapter 2 is the devastating explanation of how those ruins got there. And the answer is not what you'd expect. The poet doesn't focus on the Babylonian army. He doesn't spend his time describing siege tactics or battle strategies. Instead, he fixes his gaze squarely on God and says: he did this. God built Jerusalem. He established the temple. He filled it with his presence and called it his home. And then, piece by piece, from top to bottom, he tore it all down.

It is the most terrifying chapter in the entire book.

GOD AS DEMOLISHER

The chapter opens with the same cry as chapter 1: "Alas!" But this time the tone is different. In chapter 1, the focus was on Jerusalem's suffering, with God mentioned only a few times in passing. In chapter 2, God is the subject of nearly every sentence. He is the only one doing anything in the first ten verses. The Babylonian army barely appears. It's as if the poet has pulled back a curtain and said: forget the human armies. This is what really happened. God did this.

And the language is staggering. God has "covered Daughter Zion with the cloud of his anger." He has "hurled the splendor of Israel from heaven to earth." He has "swallowed up" all the dwellings, "torn down" the strongholds, "cut off" every source of strength. He has "burned in Jacob like a flaming fire that consumes everything around it."

Then comes the image that would have made the original audience gasp. The poet says God has acted "like an enemy." He has taken up his bow. His right hand is ready, positioned like a warrior about to fire. And then he releases the arrow, and the people who were "precious to the eye," the ones everyone treasured, fall.

Stop and think about what that means. The God who brought Israel out of Egypt with a mighty hand, the God who parted the Red Sea and sent manna from heaven and led them with a pillar of fire, that same God has now turned his hand against them. The right hand that once delivered them now destroys them. The fire that once guided them now consumes them. Every image of salvation from Israel's past is reversed and turned into an image of judgment.

This is the theological heart of Lamentations 2: God is not a distant cause of Jerusalem's suffering. He is the active agent of it. He is the demolisher of his own house.

EVERYTHING BROUGHT DOWN

The poet walks through the destruction in careful, agonizing detail. He doesn't rush. He lingers on each loss as if cataloguing the contents of a house fire.

The temple: God has "laid waste his dwelling like a garden booth," as carelessly as someone tearing down a temporary shelter after a harvest. He has "rejected his altar and abandoned his sanctuary." The altar was the most important part of the temple, the place where sacrifices were offered to maintain the relationship between God and his people. For God to reject his own altar was to reject the very system he had put in place for his people to come to him.

The walls and gates: God "stretched out a measuring line" against the city wall, the same way a builder measures before construction. But this time the measuring line was for destruction. He measured how to tear it down as carefully as he once measured how to build it up. The gates sank into the ground. The ramparts crumbled.

The leaders—the king, the princes, the priests, and the prophets—are all gone. The king is in exile. The priests have no temple to serve in. The prophets receive no word from God. This silence is devastating. For centuries, God had spoken to his people through priests and prophets. Now the prophets "no longer find visions from the Lord." God has gone quiet, and that silence is itself a form of judgment.

Throughout these verses, there is a relentless downward movement. The splendor of Israel is cast "from heaven to earth." The kingdom is brought "down to the ground." The gates "sink into the ground." The elders sit on the ground. The young women bow their heads to the ground. Everything that was once lifted up, celebrated, and exalted is brought low. The city that reached toward heaven is pushed into the dust.

CHILDREN IN THEIR MOTHERS' ARMS

At verse 11, something changes. The poet stops describing and starts feeling. Up to this point, he's been a narrator, reporting the devastation in the third person. Now he shifts to first person, and the composure cracks. "My eyes fail from weeping," he says. "I am in torment within. My heart is poured out on the ground." The reason for his breakdown is specific and gut-wrenching: children are fainting in the streets of the city.

Then comes one of the most painful images in the entire Bible. Small children cry out to their mothers, "Where is bread and wine?" They collapse in the streets like wounded soldiers. And then, in a detail so devastating it's hard to read, their lives ebb away in their mothers' arms.

The poet doesn't explain this. He doesn't theologize about it. He doesn't try to make it make sense. He just describes it, and the description is enough. This is what war does. This is what siege and famine look like up close. And the poet wants you to see it, because the children dying in their mothers' arms are the most innocent victims of the whole catastrophe. Whatever sins Jerusalem committed, these babies didn't commit them.

This is the point where the poet turns to Jerusalem herself and says, with total honesty, "Your wound is as deep as the sea. Who can heal you?"

He's tried to find something to compare her pain to. He's searched for words big enough to contain her grief. And he's failed. Nothing is big enough. Her wound is bottomless, as vast and unfathomable as the ocean. No human being can heal this. The poet, who desperately wants to be a comforter, finally admits that he can't. This is beyond his ability.

THE ONES WHO FAILED HER

Before the chapter ends, the poet identifies three groups who could have helped Jerusalem but didn't.

First, the prophets. "The visions of your prophets were false and worthless," he says. "They did not expose your sin to ward off your captivity." This is a devastating indictment. God had sent prophet after prophet to warn Israel that their rebellion would lead to disaster. But the official, court-approved prophets told the people what they wanted to hear. "Everything's fine. God would never let anything bad happen to Jerusalem. The temple is here, so we're safe." They were wrong, and their lies cost the nation everything. The lesson is stark: people who tell you only what you want to hear are not your friends. The kindest thing anyone can do for you, sometimes, is tell you the truth, even when it's hard to hear.

Second, the passersby. People who walk past the ruins of Jerusalem clap their hands in mockery. "Is this the city that was called the perfection of beauty, the joy of the whole earth?" they ask. The words are borrowed from Psalm 48, a song that once celebrated Jerusalem's glory. Now those same words are thrown back as a taunt. The glory they celebrated is gone, and the spectators seem to enjoy the spectacle.

Third, the enemies. They open their mouths wide, gnash their teeth, and celebrate. "We have swallowed her up," they boast. "This is the day we have waited for!" They think they've won by their own strength. They don't realize that they were instruments in God's hand the entire time.

The poet then pulls the camera back to the big picture: "The Lord has done what he planned. He has fulfilled his word, which he decreed long ago." This was not random chaos. This was not God losing his temper. This was the fulfillment of warnings that had been given for centuries, through Moses and through every prophet after him. If you break the covenant, these curses will come. Repentance could have averted it. It never came.

POUR OUT YOUR HEART

After all this devastation, after all this unflinching description of what God has done, you might expect the chapter to end in despair. It doesn't.

Instead, the poet does something extraordinary. He turns to Jerusalem's walls, personified as a grieving mother, and tells her to cry out. Not to give up. Not to go silent. But to pray.

"Arise, cry out in the night. Pour out your heart like water in the presence of the Lord. Lift up your hands to him for the lives of your children."

This is remarkable. The same God who is described as the cause of the destruction is the same God the poet tells Jerusalem to pray to. He doesn't say, "Pray to someone else." He doesn't say, "God can't be trusted anymore." He says: pour out your heart to him. Bring your pain, your anger, your unanswerable questions, and lay them at his feet. He may be the one who wounded you, but he is also the only one who can heal you.

And Jerusalem does pray. In the final verses, she turns to God and asks the hardest question in the entire book: "Look, Lord, and consider: whom have you ever treated like this?" She describes the unthinkable horrors of the siege. She does not soften her words. She does not pretend things are better than they are. She brings the full, ugly, devastating truth before God and essentially says: explain this to me.

God does not answer. Not yet. His silence hangs over the end of the chapter like a cloud. But the fact that Jerusalem prays at all, that she still speaks to the God she believes has destroyed her, is an act of faith more profound than a thousand worship songs sung in comfortable times.

WHAT THIS MEANS FOR US

First, nothing you build is permanent except what God sustains. Jerusalem had the most beautiful temple in the ancient world. They had the promises of God, the presence of God, the worship of God. And they still lost everything, because they treated God's gifts as guarantees instead of responsibilities. No church building, no Christian tradition, no religious institution is immune to judgment if it stops being faithful to the God it claims to serve.

Second, the people who tell you hard truths are more valuable than the ones who tell you what you want to hear. The false prophets made Jerusalem feel safe. The real prophets, people like Jeremiah, were ignored and persecuted because their message was uncomfortable. Pay attention to the people in your life who love you enough to be honest with you, even when it stings. They might be the ones saving you from something far worse down the road.

Third, you can bring your hardest questions to God. Lamentations 2 doesn't end with a neat answer. It ends with a question and a silence. But it also ends with prayer. The poet doesn't tell Jerusalem to stop talking to God because God let her down. He tells her to talk louder. If you're confused about something God has allowed in your life, if you're angry or hurt or struggling to make sense of what's happened, don't walk away from God. Walk toward him. Pour out your heart like water. He can take it.

Fourth, God's silence is not the same as God's absence. The prophets received no visions. God did not speak. But the book of Lamentations itself is proof that God had not abandoned his people forever. These poems were preserved, treasured, and read aloud by the very community that survived the destruction. The silence was real, but it was not permanent. Silence is sometimes the space where God is preparing to do something new.

TALKING POINTS

1. **The poet describes God acting "like an enemy" toward his own people.** Why do you think the Bible includes such raw and uncomfortable descriptions of God? What does it tell us about the kind of honesty God allows in our relationship with him?

2. **The false prophets told Jerusalem what they wanted to hear instead of what they needed to hear.** Can you think of situations where it's tempting to only listen to people who agree with you? Why is it important to have people in your life who will tell you the truth, even when it's uncomfortable?

3. **The poet tells Jerusalem to "pour out your heart like water in the presence of the Lord."** What does that image mean to you? What would it look like to bring your emotions to God that honestly, not filtering or cleaning them up first?

4. **God's silence at the end of the chapter is striking.** Have you ever felt like God was silent when you really needed to

hear from him? How did you handle that? What helped you keep going during that quiet season?

5. **The chapter shows us that God's gifts, like the temple, the city, and the leaders, can be lost if people treat them carelessly.** What are some blessings in your own life that you might be taking for granted? How can you be more intentional about being faithful with what God has given you?

The ruins are still smoking. God is still silent. The questions hanging in the air have no answers yet. But right in the middle of the darkest book in the Bible, the poet is about to say something that will change everything.

Turn the page.

7

HOPE IN THE DARKNESS

Daniel Defoe's *Robinson Crusoe* is one of the most famous survival stories ever written. After a shipwreck, Crusoe washes up on a deserted island with nothing. No shelter. No food. No tools. No other people. He's completely alone in a place that seems determined to kill him. The early chapters of the book are filled with despair. Crusoe is terrified, exhausted, and certain that he is going to die. He feels abandoned by everyone, including God. He rages against his circumstances. He collapses into self-pity. He can barely find the will to get up in the morning.

But then something shifts. Crusoe doesn't get rescued. His circumstances don't change. What changes is the way he sees them. He starts to make a list of the things he still has. He's alive. He made it to shore. There's fresh water on the island. There are animals he can hunt. He has tools he salvaged from the wreck. He has his mind and his hands and his health.

None of that erases the fact that he's stranded. None of it fixes the shipwreck. But it gives him something to stand on. He starts building. He makes a shelter, then a fence, then a garden. He begins reading the Bible he found in the wreckage, and for the first time in his life, he starts to pray, not out of habit but out of genuine need. The despair doesn't disappear overnight. But something takes root inside it: a stubborn, fragile, hard-won hope.

Lamentations 3 is the Robinson Crusoe chapter of the Bible's darkest book. It's the moment when a man who has been beaten down by suffering, who has accused God of treating him like an enemy, who has declared that all his hope is destroyed, suddenly stops, looks around, and remembers something that changes everything.

What he remembers is this: God's love has not run out.

THE MAN WHO SUFFERED

Lamentations 3 opens with a single voice. Not the grieving woman of chapters 1–2. This time it's a man, and he speaks in the first person: "I am the man who has seen affliction."

For eighteen verses, he describes what God has done to him, and the images are brutal. God has driven him into darkness. God has walled him in like a prisoner and refused to hear his prayers. God has been like a bear lying in wait, like a lion crouching in the shadows, ready to pounce. God has bent his bow and made the man the target of his arrows. God has broken his teeth with gravel, trampled him in the dust, and stripped away everything good in his life.

If you're reading this and thinking, "This sounds a lot like what Jerusalem said in chapters 1–2," you're right. The man's suffering mirrors the city's suffering. His story is their story. He represents the whole community, the people of God who have been crushed by the Babylonian destruction and who feel as though God himself turned against them.

By the end of verse 18, the man hits rock bottom. "My splendor is gone," he says, "and all that I had hoped from the Lord." He has lost everything, including his ability to see any way forward. Hope is not just fading. In his mind, it's dead.

This is the lowest point in the entire book.

THE TURN

And then, in verse 19, something begins to shift. It's not dramatic. There are no angels or miraculous signs. The man simply starts talking to himself. He says, in effect, "I remember my suffering. I remember the bitterness. My soul is downcast when I think about it." That doesn't sound like progress. It sounds like he's just repeating his misery.

But then comes verse 21: "Yet this I call to mind, and therefore I have hope."

Wait. Hope? Where did that come from? He just said his hope was destroyed. He just spent eighteen verses describing a God who seemed to be systematically dismantling his life. What could he possibly have remembered that would produce hope in the middle of all that?

The answer comes in the very next verses, and they are the most famous lines in the entire book of Lamentations: "Because of the Lord's great love, we are not consumed, for his compassions never fail. They are new every morning; great is your faithfulness."

Read that again slowly. Let it sink in.

The man has not been rescued. His city is still in ruins. His people are still in exile. His prayers still seem to go unanswered. Nothing in his circumstances has changed. But something in his perspective has. He has remembered something about who God is, and that memory has become a lifeline.

What he remembers is not a single event. It's a pattern. Over and over in Israel's history, God had shown faithful love to his people. Even when they sinned. Even when they broke the covenant. Even when he punished them, his love outlasted his anger. The golden calf incident in Exodus, where God could have destroyed the entire nation but instead renewed his covenant with them because he is "compassionate and gracious, slow to anger, abounding in love and faithfulness." That's what the man is reaching back to. Not wishful thinking. Not denial. History. God's track record.

And the most remarkable word in the passage might be "new." His compassions are new every morning. Not recycled. Not leftover. Fresh. Every single day, no matter how terrible the day before was, God's mercy shows up again. The man can't see the end of his suffering. He doesn't know when things will get better. But he knows that tomorrow morning, God's compassion will be there again, as sure as the sunrise.

THE CENTER OF THE BOOK

Here's something remarkable about where these verses fall. The book of Lamentations has five chapters. Chapter 3 is the middle chapter. And within chapter 3, the declaration that God "does not willingly bring affliction or grief to anyone" sits at the very center of the poem. In a book that is carefully, deliberately structured from beginning to end, the poet has placed this truth about God's character at the exact heart of everything.

Think about what that means. Lamentations is a book of grief, anger, confusion, and unanswered questions. But at the very center of all that pain, like a diamond buried in rock, is this: God does not enjoy your suffering. His punishment is real, but it is not his heart's desire. His anger is temporary. His love is permanent.

The poet puts it this way: "Though he brings grief, he will show compassion, so great is his unfailing love. For he does not willingly bring affliction or grief to anyone."

That word "willingly" is important. A more literal translation would be "from his heart." God does not afflict people from his heart. Judgment is something God does reluctantly, after centuries of warning and patience. It is his response to sin, not his default mode of relating to his people. In his innermost being, God is full of compassion and faithful love. That is who he truly is.

This doesn't erase the suffering. It doesn't make the ruins of Jerusalem suddenly okay. But it changes the meaning of the suffering. If God's anger is temporary and his love is permanent, then the worst season of your life is not the final chapter of your story. There is something on the other side of the pain.

ADVICE FOR SUFFERERS

After the man recovers his hope, he turns to the people around him and offers some practical wisdom about how to survive seasons of suffering.

"It is good to wait quietly for the salvation of the Lord," he says. This doesn't mean sitting silently and pretending everything is fine. Throughout Lamentations, the people cry out, weep, and bring their raw complaints to God. The "quiet waiting" the man recommends is not the absence of prayer but the presence of trust. It's the kind of waiting that says, "I don't know when this will end, but I believe the God who brought me here will bring me through."

He also says something surprising: "It is good for a man to bear the yoke while he is young." This isn't a celebration of suffering. Nobody in Lamentations thinks pain is fun. The point is practical: if you have to go through hard things, the strength and resilience of youth give you a better chance of bearing the weight. And suffering, as painful as it is, can teach you things about yourself and about God that comfort never could.

Then the man asks a question that brings the whole chapter into focus: "Why should the living complain when punished for their sins?" This is not meant to shut down grief. The entire book of Lamentations is proof that God welcomes honest complaint. But the man is making a distinction between two kinds of response to suffering. One says, "I don't deserve this, and God has no right to do this to me." The other says, "I have sinned, God's judgment is just, but his love is greater than his anger, and so I will wait for him to show mercy." The man is calling the people toward the second response.

THE PRAYER THAT FOLLOWS

And the people listen. In verse 40, the man calls the community to examine their ways and return to the Lord. "Let us lift up our hearts and our hands to God in heaven," he says. And then they pray together—not a polished, comfortable prayer, but a raw, honest, anguished prayer that accuses God of refusing to listen, that describes the devastation in unflinching terms, and that still somehow manages to keep talking to the God they believe has wounded them.

The man himself commits to weeping without stopping until God looks down from heaven and sees what has happened. He doesn't set a timer on his grief. He doesn't say, "I'll be sad for a week and then I'll move on." He says he will keep weeping, keep praying, keep crying out until God responds.

In the final section of the chapter, the man tells his own story of deliverance. He was in a pit. His enemies were closing in. He was about to be swallowed up. And in that moment, he called out to God, and God said, "Do not fear." God came near. God took up his case. God redeemed his life.

The man offers his own rescue as a model for what the community can hope for. His story isn't finished. His enemies are still out there. But God showed up when he called, and that changes everything. If God did it for him, God can do it for them.

WHAT THIS MEANS FOR US

First, hope doesn't require a change in circumstances. The man in Lamentations 3 found hope not because his situation improved but because he remembered something true about God's character. When you're in a dark season, you don't have to wait for things to get better before you're allowed to hope. You can hope right now, in the middle of the mess, because of who God is.

Second, God's mercy is new every morning. This might be the most comforting sentence in the entire Old Testament.

It means that no matter how badly yesterday went, today is a fresh start. You don't have to carry the weight of every past failure into every new day. God's compassion resets. Every sunrise is proof that he hasn't given up on you.

Third, God's anger is temporary, but his love is permanent. If you've ever felt like God was angry with you, like you'd messed up too badly to be forgiven, Lamentations 3 says otherwise. God may discipline, but he doesn't do it because he enjoys it. He does it because he's trying to bring you back. And when the discipline has done its work, what's waiting on the other side is mercy, not more punishment.

Fourth, honest grief and genuine hope can exist in the same heart at the same time. The man in this chapter weeps and hopes. He accuses God and trusts God. He laments and prays. These aren't contradictions. They're what real faith looks like in real suffering. You don't have to choose between being honest about your pain and trusting that God is good. You can do both.

TALKING POINTS

1. **The man says, "His compassions are new every morning."** What does it mean to you that God's mercy resets every day? How might remembering this change the way you start your mornings, especially on days when you're carrying guilt or discouragement from the day before?

2. **The turning point in the chapter comes when the man deliberately "calls to mind" something true about God. He chooses to remember.** Why do you think it's important to actively remind yourself of what you know about God, especially

when your emotions are telling you something different? What are some ways you could practice doing that?

3. **The poet says God does not "willingly" or "from his heart" bring affliction.** How does knowing that God takes no pleasure in your pain change the way you think about hard seasons in your life? How is that different from saying God doesn't care about what happens to you?

4. **The man offers his own story of deliverance as a model for the community. He says, in effect, "God rescued me, and he can rescue you too."** Has someone ever shared their story of getting through a difficult time in a way that gave you hope for your own situation? Why do you think personal stories are so powerful?

5. **Lamentations 3 places hope at the very center of a book filled with grief. It doesn't ignore the grief or pretend it doesn't exist. It just refuses to let grief have the last word.** What does it look like in your own life to hold on to hope without pretending that everything is fine?

Hope has been found, but the story of Jerusalem's suffering is not over. The poet still has more to say about the devastation, and the hardest question of all, what comes next, is still waiting to be answered.

Turn the page.

8

PICKING UP THE PIECES

Dunkirk is not the kind of war movie where the heroes charge forward with guns blazing and win the day. It's the opposite.

In the spring of 1940, hundreds of thousands of British and Allied soldiers were trapped on the beaches of Dunkirk, France. The German army had pushed them to the edge of the sea. There was nowhere left to go. The soldiers stood in long, silent lines on the sand, staring out at the water, waiting for ships that might never come. Enemy planes screamed overhead, bombing the beach. Torpedoes sank the rescue boats. Every hour that passed felt like a countdown to the end.

The film doesn't give you grand speeches or dramatic heroics. It gives you something harder to watch: ordinary people surviving one moment at a time, not knowing if the next moment will be their last. Soldiers hiding in a beached boat, listening to bullets punch through the hull. A teenager on a civilian pleasure boat heading into a war zone because someone has to help. Men standing waist-deep in cold water, holding their rifles above their heads, watching the horizon for rescue.

And then, at the very end, the little boats appear. Hundreds of civilian vessels, fishing boats and yachts and ferries, crossing the English Channel to bring the soldiers home. It's not a victory. Dunkirk was a massive military defeat. But the evacuation itself was a kind of miracle: survival against impossible odds, rescue when all hope seemed lost.

The last two chapters of Lamentations feel a lot like that beach at Dunkirk. The destruction is over, but the suffering hasn't stopped. The survivors are picking through the rubble of their lives, trying to figure out how to keep going in a world that has been completely torn apart. And at the very end, they do the only thing they can: they look toward the horizon and pray for rescue.

WHEN GOLD BECOMES DIRT

Lamentations 4 opens with the same cry of anguish that began chapters 1–2: "Alas!" And then the poet delivers one of the most devastating images in the entire book. "How the gold has lost its luster, the fine gold become dull! The sacred gems are scattered at the head of every street."

At first you think he's talking about the gold and precious stones from the temple, now lying in the rubble like garbage. But in the very next verse you realize: the "gold" is not metal. It's people. The precious sons of Zion, once valued as worth their weight in gold, are now treated like cheap pottery, broken and thrown away.

This is the theme that runs through all of Lamentations 4: everything precious has become worthless. The wealthy who once ate the finest food are now scavenging in trash heaps.

Leaders who once looked healthy and strong are now unrecognizable, their skin shriveled and dark with malnutrition. The normal bonds of human society have broken down under the weight of famine so severe that it has driven people to do things too terrible to describe.

The poet says something startling: Jerusalem's suffering was worse than Sodom's. Sodom's punishment came in an instant, a flash of fire and it was over. Jerusalem's punishment came slowly, through months of siege and starvation, a lingering death that stripped the people of their dignity before it took their lives. The poet concludes grimly that it would have been better to die quickly by a sword than to waste away from hunger.

WHY THIS HAPPENED

In the middle of the chapter, the poet gives the most focused explanation in the entire book for why God allowed this catastrophe.

He points directly at the leaders: the prophets and the priests. These were the people responsible for guiding the nation spiritually. They were supposed to teach God's law, speak God's truth, and call the people back when they wandered. Instead, they did the opposite. The prophets gave false visions. The priests committed injustice. They silenced the people who tried to speak the truth. The poet describes them as having "shed the blood of the righteous," a reference either to literal violence against faithful prophets like Jeremiah or to the spiritual devastation caused by their lies.

The consequences were fitting. The religious leaders who were supposed to be the most pure became the most unclean.

They wandered the streets covered in guilt, rejected by their own people. Even foreign nations refused to take them in. The leaders who led the people astray ended up with nowhere to go.

There is a hard lesson here, and it's one that applies far beyond ancient Jerusalem. When the people responsible for spiritual leadership fail, everyone suffers. A preacher who tells people what they want to hear instead of what they need to hear, a teacher who ignores the truth to avoid conflict, a leader who cares more about power than about faithfulness—these are the "little foxes" from Song of Songs grown into wolves. Bad leadership doesn't just hurt the leaders. It pulls entire communities down with them.

A SURPRISING WORD OF HOPE

After twenty verses of relentless darkness, something unexpected happens. A voice breaks in, and it sounds like a prophet delivering an oracle from God.

The voice addresses Edom, the neighboring nation that had rejoiced over Jerusalem's fall and plundered the city in its weakness. "Rejoice while you can," the voice says, dripping with irony. "The cup of God's judgment that Jerusalem has drunk will be passed to you next."

And then, the most hopeful words in all of Lamentations 4: "Your punishment will be completed, Daughter Zion. He will not keep you in exile any longer."

This is enormous. After four chapters of devastation, after children dying in the streets and temples burning and leaders fleeing and gold turning to dust, the poet says: this will end. The exile has a limit. God's anger has a boundary. The punishment, as terrible as it is, will be "completed," which means it will be finished, done, over.

Remember what the man said in chapter 3: "He will not reject forever." Here is the proof. Even in the darkest chapter yet, the poet refuses to let the darkness have the last word.

THE FINAL PRAYER

Lamentations 5 is different from everything that came before it. The previous four chapters moved between narration, description, and prayer. Chapter 5 is nothing but prayer. From first verse to last, the people of Jerusalem are speaking directly to God.

It begins with a single desperate request: "Remember, Lord, what has happened to us. Look, and see our disgrace."

Then the people pour out their situation. Their inheritance, the land God gave them, has been taken by foreigners. They are orphans and widows. They have to pay money for water that comes from their own wells and wood from their own forests. They are worked like slaves in their own homeland. The elders no longer sit at the city gates. The young men no longer play music. Joy has disappeared from their hearts, and dancing has turned to mourning.

Verse 16 contains a confession that has been building throughout the entire book: "Woe to us, for we have sinned." No excuses. No blame-shifting. No arguing that the punishment was unfair. Just a plain, honest acknowledgment: we did this. We sinned, and we are living in the wreckage of our choices.

And then comes the detail that breaks the poet's heart more than anything else: "Mount Zion lies desolate, with jackals prowling over it." The temple mount, once the place where heaven and earth met, where God's presence dwelt among his people, is now a ruin inhabited by wild animals. Of all the losses catalogued in this book, this one is the heaviest. Because the temple wasn't just a building. It was the physical sign that God was with his people. Its destruction felt like the death of the relationship itself.

RESTORE US

And yet.

The people don't end in despair. They end in prayer. And their prayer builds to one of the most important declarations in the entire book: "You, Lord, reign forever; your throne endures from generation to generation."

The temple is gone. The city is gone. The king is gone. But God is still on his throne. His reign hasn't ended. His power hasn't diminished. The Babylonians may have torn down every structure in Jerusalem, but they cannot touch the throne of God. And because God still reigns, it is still possible to pray. It is still possible to hope.

Then comes the aching question: "Why do you always forget us? Why do you forsake us so long?"

This is not a statement of unbelief. It's the kind of question that only someone who deeply believes in God would ask. If God didn't reign, if he didn't care, there would be no point asking why he seems absent. The question itself is proof of faith.

And finally, the last prayer of the book: "Restore us to yourself, Lord, and we will be restored. Renew our days as of old."

The people aren't asking for their stuff back. They aren't praying for gold or buildings or military power. They're asking for the one thing that matters: their relationship with God. Restore us *to yourself*. Bring us back to you. That's the heart of the prayer, and it's the heart of the entire book.

THE UNFINISHED ENDING

Lamentations doesn't end neatly. The very last line is not a declaration of faith but a haunted question: "Unless you have utterly rejected us and are angry with us beyond measure."

That's it. That's how the book ends. Not with a resolution but with a question hanging in the air. Have you rejected us completely? Is this really the end?

It's an uncomfortable way to close a book. We want a tidy conclusion. We want God to answer. But Lamentations refuses to give us that, and there's a reason. The people praying this prayer are still in the ruins. They haven't been restored yet. The rescue boats haven't appeared on the horizon. All they have is a prayer and a God who, as far as they can tell, hasn't answered yet.

The Jewish tradition understood the tension of this ending so well that when Lamentations is read aloud in synagogues, the congregation repeats verse 21 after reading verse 22: "Restore us to yourself, Lord, and we will be restored." They refuse to let the book's final sound be a question about rejection. The last word they speak is a prayer for restoration.

And from where we stand, on this side of the cross and the empty tomb, we know something the poet couldn't have known. God did answer that prayer. Not on their timetable and not in the way they expected. But the exile ended. The people returned. The temple was rebuilt. And centuries later, God himself entered the ruins of the human condition in the person of Jesus, the ultimate answer to every prayer for restoration the Bible has ever recorded.

WHAT THIS MEANS FOR US

First, suffering reveals what we truly value. When everything was stripped away from Jerusalem, the people didn't cry out for their gold or their palaces. They cried out for God. Suffering has a way of burning away the things that don't matter and exposing the things that do. When your life falls apart, pay attention to what you reach for. That will tell you what you really care about.

Second, bad leadership has real consequences. The prophets and priests who failed Jerusalem didn't just make a personal mistake. Their failure brought an entire community to ruin. If you're in any kind of leadership, whether as a team captain, an older sibling, a class officer, or just a friend people look up to, take that responsibility seriously. The people who follow you are trusting you to point them in the right direction.

Third, it's okay to pray without having answers. The people in Lamentations 5 don't understand why God has allowed their suffering to go on so long. They say so honestly. But they pray anyway. You don't have to figure out what God is doing before you talk to him about it. Bring your confusion. Bring your unanswered questions. Bring your "why." He's still on his throne, and he's still listening.

Fourth, the most important thing you can ask God for is himself. "Restore us to yourself." Not "restore our comfort" or "restore our success." The deepest need of the human heart is not for things but for relationship with the God who made us.

Everything else can be lost and rebuilt. But if you lose your connection to God, nothing else will fill the gap.

TALKING POINTS

1. **The poet says that Jerusalem's "gold" turned out to be her children, treated as worthless pottery.** What are the things in your life that might look ordinary on the outside but are actually the most precious things you have? How can you make sure you treat them accordingly?

2. **Lamentations blames the prophets and priests for failing to tell the truth.** Why is it so tempting for leaders to tell people what they want to hear instead of what they need to hear? How can you become the kind of person who values honesty, even when it's uncomfortable?

3. **The book ends with an unanswered question rather than a neat conclusion.** Why do you think the poet chose to end this way? Have you ever been in a situation where you had to live with unanswered questions? What helped you keep going?

4. **The people's final prayer is "Restore us to yourself." They don't ask for comfort or wealth; they ask for relationship with God.** What does that tell you about what matters most in life? If you could ask God for one thing right now, what would it be, and why?

5. **From our perspective, we know that God eventually answered Jerusalem's prayer through the return from exile and ultimately through Jesus.** How does knowing the end of the story change the way you read Lamentations? How might it change the way you think about the unanswered prayers in your own life?

The poems are finished. The grief has been spoken. The prayers have been offered. But the story of Song of Songs and Lamentations isn't complete until we step back and see how these two very different books fit together in the larger story of God's love for his people.

Turn the page.

CONCLUSION

We started this book with a question: what's the strongest emotion you've ever felt?

Now, having walked through the Song of Songs and Lamentations together, I want to ask you a different question: what kind of God allows both of these books into his Bible?

Think about what we've read. A love poem so honest it makes you blush, where a young woman boldly declares her desire and a young man calls her the most beautiful woman alive. Poetry about springtime and gardens, about gazelles on the mountains and lilies in the valleys, about two ordinary people whose love for each other burns with a flame that even death cannot extinguish.

And then, without any transition, without any warning, a funeral. A city in ashes. Children dying in the streets. A poet so broken that he can barely find words big enough to hold his grief. Prayers that go unanswered. Silence from heaven. A final desperate cry: "Restore us to yourself, Lord, and we will be restored."

The same God inspired both books. The same God said, "Put this love poetry in my Word," and "Put this grief poetry in my Word." He didn't choose one and reject the other. He kept them both, side by side, as if to say: I am the God of all of this. The joy and the sorrow. The celebration and the devastation. The garden and the ruins. I am present in every room of your life, not just the ones that feel holy.

That matters more than you might realize.

WHAT WE'VE LEARNED

Here's what these two books have taught us.

From the Song of Songs, we learned that love is God's idea. He created it. He celebrates it. He designed it to be something so beautiful that even heaven throws a party when it's done right. We learned that real love sees past insecurity and speaks life into people. That the deepest romance is built on genuine friendship. That love requires patience, because the most valuable things in life cannot be rushed. That love is tested by carelessness and comfort, and that grace can rebuild what neglect has broken. And at the summit of it all, we heard the woman declare what the entire Bible confirms: love is as strong as death. Its flame is the very flame of God. No flood can drown it. No fortune can buy it. No power on earth can put it out.

From Lamentations, we learned that grief has a place in faith. That you don't have to clean up your emotions before you bring them to God. That honest pain and honest trust can live in the same heart at the same time. We learned that sin has real consequences, but consequences don't cancel out compassion. That God's silence is not the same as God's absence. That the people who tell you hard truths are more valuable than the ones who tell you what you want to hear. And right at the center of the darkest book in the Bible, we found a diamond buried in the rock: "His compassions never fail. They are new every morning. Great is your faithfulness."

Two books. Two extremes of human experience. One God who refuses to be absent from either.

WHERE IT ALL POINTS

But here's the thing that ties everything together, the thread that runs through both books and out the other side into the rest of the Bible's story.

The love that Song of Songs celebrates, a love as strong as death, was perfectly embodied in a person. His name is Jesus.

Jesus is the one whose love is literally stronger than death. He proved it. He walked into the grave on a Friday afternoon, and he walked out of it on a Sunday morning. The flame that Song of Songs describes, the fire that no flood can quench, burned brightest on the cross, where the Son of God gave his life for people who had turned their backs on him. Charlotte gave her life for Wilbur. Westley crossed oceans for Buttercup. But Jesus crossed the distance between heaven and earth, between holiness and sin, between life and death, for you.

And the grief that Lamentations voices, the anguished cry of a people who feel abandoned by God, was answered in that same person. When Jerusalem prayed, "Restore us to yourself," God's answer was not a program or a policy. It was a baby in a manger who grew up to be a man on a cross. Jesus entered the ruins. He didn't stand at a safe distance and offer advice. He walked into the ashes of the human condition and took our devastation onto himself. He wept at a friend's grave. He sweat blood in a garden. He cried out from the cross, "My God, my God, why have you forsaken me?" words that could have come straight from the book of Lamentations.

The God who seemed silent at the end of Lamentations was not absent. He was preparing the greatest answer to prayer the world has ever seen. The exile ended. The people returned. The temple was rebuilt. And then, centuries later, God himself moved into the neighborhood, not in a building made of stone but in a body made of flesh. The presence that once filled the tabernacle and the temple now walked the streets of Jerusalem in sandals.

Song of Songs asks: is there a love strong enough to conquer death?

Lamentations asks: is there a God faithful enough to restore what sin has destroyed?

The answer to both questions is the same. Yes. His name is Jesus.

WHAT NOW?

So what do you do with all of this?

First, don't be afraid of your emotions. You are going to feel things in your life that are bigger than you know how to handle. You're going to experience joy that makes you want to shout, and grief that makes you want to disappear. You're going to fall in love and get your heart broken. You're going to win things and lose things and wonder what any of it means. The Bible says: bring it all to God. Every feeling. Every question. Every celebration and every complaint. God is not intimidated by your emotions. He made them.

Second, guard what matters most. The Song of Songs taught us that love is worth protecting. The locked garden wasn't a prison. It was a treasure chest. The things you guard most carefully, your heart, your character, your closest relationships, your faith, are the things that will mean the most when the time comes to share them. In a world that tells you to give everything away as fast as possible, wisdom says: wait. Protect. Invest. The harvest is coming.

Third, keep talking to God, especially when it's hard. Lamentations taught us that the most profound act of faith is not a worship song sung in a comfortable room. It's a prayer screamed from the ashes. If you're confused, tell him. If you're angry, tell him. If you feel abandoned, tell him. The people of Lamentations never stopped talking to God, even when he seemed to have stopped listening. And in the end, he answered. He always answers. Sometimes the answer takes longer than we'd like. Sometimes it looks different than we expected. But the God who heard Jerusalem's cry hears yours too.

Fourth, remember that your story is not over. If you had stopped reading Song of Songs after chapter 3, you would have missed the greatest declaration about love ever written. If you had stopped reading Lamentations after chapter 2, you would have missed the hope at the center of the book. If you had closed the Bible after Good Friday, you would have missed Easter. Whatever chapter you're living in right now, it is not the last one. God is still writing. The best part may still be ahead.

THE LAST WORD

The Song of Songs ends with an invitation: "Come away, my

beloved." The voice of love calling us closer, always closer, never finished, never satisfied with distance.

Lamentations ends with a prayer: "Restore us to yourself, Lord." The voice of a broken people reaching for the only one who can put them back together.

Both voices are still speaking today. Love is still calling. The broken are still praying. And the God who kindled the flame and who sits with us in the ashes is still faithful.

His mercies are new every morning.

His love is as strong as death.

And he is not finished with your story yet.